CONTAINER GARDENING

Grow Organic Vegetables and Organic Herbs with Container Gardening

JOY LOUIS

©Copyright 2015 Great Reads Publishing, LLC - All rights reserved.

This document is geared towards providing exact and reliable information in regards to the topic and issue covered. The publication is sold with the idea that the publisher is not required to render accounting, officially permitted, or otherwise, qualified services. If advice is necessary, legal or professional, a practiced individual in the profession should be ordered.

From a Declaration of Principles which was accepted and approved equally by a Committee of the American Bar Association and a Committee of Publishers and Associations.

In no way is it legal to reproduce, duplicate, or transmit any part of this document in either electronic means or in printed format. Recording of this publication is strictly prohibited and any storage of this document is not allowed unless with written permission from the publisher. All rights reserved.

The information provided herein is stated to be truthful and consistent, in that any liability, in terms of inattention or otherwise, by any usage or abuse of any policies, processes, or directions contained within is the solitary and utter responsibility of the recipient reader. Under no circumstances will any legal responsibility or blame be held against the publisher for any reparation, damages, or monetary loss due to the information herein, either directly or indirectly.

The information herein is offered for informational purposes solely, and is universal as so. The presentation of the information is without contract or any type of guarantee assurance.

The trademarks that are used are without any consent, and the publication of the trademark is without permission or backing by the trademark owner. All trademarks and brands within this book are for clarifying purposes only and are the owned by the owners themselves, not affiliated with this document.

WAIT! – DO YOU LIKE FREE BOOKS?

My FREE Gift to You!! As a way to say Thank You for downloading my book, I'd like to offer you more FREE BOOKS! Each time we release a NEW book, we offer it first to a small number of people as a test - drive. Because of your commitment here in downloading my book, I'd love for you to be a part of this group. You can join easily here → http://gardening-mastery.com/

Table of Contents

Chapter 1	Container Gardening	5
Chapter 2	Choosing the Containers for your Garden	9
Chapter 3	Container Garden Essentials	14
Chapter 4	The Right Soil is Crucial	17
Chapter 5	Homemade Potting Soil Recipe	20
Chapter 6	Planting a Container Garden	24
Chapter 7	Vegetables in a Container	27
Chapter 8	Seeds in a Container Garden	29
Chapter 9	Caring for Your Container Garden	31
Chapter 10	Dealing with Container Garden Problems	34
Chapter 11	Mistakes to Avoid	37
Chapter 12	Indoor Container Gardens	43
Chapter 13	10 Container Garden Ideas	48
Chapter 14	Tips for Successful Container Gardening	57
Conclusion		61

Chapter 1

Container Gardening

Small scale gardens mean frequent upkeep. You will need to water the plants more often since there is a limited amount of soil in the container. Remember to fertilize the plants in container gardens more often than plants in a bare earth garden. If you don't have any containers, you might have to invest more than you would like in purchasing artsy containers. (Or look around your home and start a container garden in a large bowl, teapot, milk jug, or anything else). All these disadvantages are really nothing. Container gardening brings balance to your life, soul and your garden.

Container gardening dates back thousands of years. The Roman were famous for their gardens, and in Egyptian and Oriental homes plants of every size and color were used to provide ambiance. The Hanging Gardens of Babylon, were one of the Seven Wonders of the World, and their legendary beauty was said to be mind-boggling.

There are thousands of chronicles discussing ancient Indian container gardening using medicinal and edible plants. Religious ceremonies often used container gardening as a way to show respect. In Athens, women placed earthen pots planted with fennel and lettuce as well as wheat and barley around the statue of Adonis. They believed it would bring them a lover. Container gardening brings the magic of planting, harvesting, and enjoyment to a variety of situations. If you are a flower garden lover, container gardening is the perfect way to "worship" gardening.

Overflowing pots, tubs, barrels and funky containers add appeal to a garden. Container gardens are practical. It is ideal for those with little to no gardening space or those who want to add architectural interest to an already growing flower or vegetable bed. Container gardens are perfect for growing a variety of vegetable crops. You can do a unique herb garden with basil, chives, thyme and other herbs and sit that container in a sunny spot right outside the kitchen door.

Container Gardening

Container gardening adds versatility to gardens that are large or those that are small. They provide instant color and a focal point in the garden. You can use containers to tie the house to the garden. Place containers on the ground or a pedestal. Mount them on a windowsill or hang them from the porch. Matching containers on either side of your front walkway serves as a welcome sign, and containers on a patio add color and ambiance to an outside sitting area.

Clusters of pots can contain a collection of flowers and plants. You can plant just about any plant in a container. How about your houseplants? In decorative pots, they summer outdoors in the garden and make a great addition to your outside space. Add a window box or a hanging basket to your home, and you have instant appeal.

Container gardens are great for beginning gardeners. It is a relative inexpensive hobby, and you can watch your creations grow. Container gardening provides an opportunity to save seeds and trade with other gardeners or just create future plants for yourself. Great advantages of container gardens; less back pain and you can just adjust the height of the pots to your preference.

You can move your garden around to different areas if you grow things in a container. You might need to bring your plants indoors during cool months, which makes an awesome addition to inside environments. There are so many varieties of containers available that you can design a very artistic garden. A couple of huge advantages to container gardening for many gardeners? You won't have pets trampling through your container garden, and weeds tend to stay on the ground rather than in the container. You can see insects, replant when you want, change the theme of the container garden, and so many more advantages.

Chapter 2

CHOOSING THE CONTAINERS FOR YOUR GARDEN

Think outside the norm - container gardening at its most gorgeous (www.southernliving.com)

It is so fun to pick out the containers for your garden. Think outside your normal ceramic or terracotta pot. One enthusiastic neighbor down the street uses a row boat each year for her plantings. Pumpkins, marigolds, tomatoes and other unrecognizable flower plants grow in this boat. It is very eclectic, and she gets her picture in the gardening news of the local newspaper every year. Another friend plants pumpkins in large broken pieces of pottery. She trains the plants to grow up and over an unsightly fence. Not only does this create a fantastic look to her fence, but she has pumpkins for Halloween decorations.

Some tips and tricks to remember about container gardens, light colored containers are less likely to absorb heat. They will keep roots cool during warm months. Put heavy or oversized pots and containers on a platform with wheels. Wheels will make it easier to move the container when you need to and where you want.

When planting in containers remember that you need to match the size of the plant to the container. A small pot will hinder the growth of full sized tomato or lavender plant. Tomatoes need stakes and room to grow to their full potential. Make sure the container anchors the weight of the plant when heavy laden with warm, ripe fruits. Anchoring your vegetable and large flower plans will keep the plants from breaking the stems and rotting on the ground.

You may not want to plant garlic in an oversized pot. Garlic will grow much better in a shallow container. A friend with a small condo space planted peas in one container, cucumbers in another, garlic and tomatoes in another. She placed the pots against the deck rails and trellised them. The effect was very adorable.

Experiment placing different plants near each other when creating your container garden. Mix and match plants of different types and sizes. Try a tall plant in a large container or a vine that tumbles over the side of a lower container. You can plant vegetable and flowers together in a pot or use different styles and colors of pots grouped together to compliment your flowers and vegetables. A very nice arrangement down the street was a grouping of cherry tomatoes, chili peppers, and purple petunias. Pink begonias and leafy coleus set off the very unusual arrangement.

Make your containers by finding things that can hold dirt. Anything can be a container. A new meaning for the "pot" is a toilet cistern in a greenhouse garden. How about your old tea kettle. You can reuse it as a watering can or recycle into a planter. Plant in an old urn or an old fashioned water pitcher to use as a centerpiece on an outside table. Colanders are perfect used as a container. Plant vegetables, flowers or herbs in a colander; you have instant holes for drainage.

Before using any old thing for a container, check the material of the skin. Is it safe and the surface porous? Terracotta pots are fun, but extremely porous and absorb and leach water and fertilizers through the surface.

Stay away from pots contaminated with lead or asbestos. Lead is a naturally occurring metal, but it is poison to all forms of life. Avoid old containers coated with lead paint or building materials that may have asbestos remnants.

If you want to renovate an interesting piece of furniture from a salvage shop, find out the age of the materials first. Don't use painted materials for a garden planter if you can't determine if they are safe. Use them as a decoration without a plant, but maybe as a complementing accessory

If you have something that you love, and want to use it as a container for your garden, just get creative. Use a liner or as a cachepot or a decorative container used to conceal a smaller pot. One pot inside a larger pot is called double potting, and helps keep your plants safe.

Find the lettuce! Unique boxes and buckets filled with edibles (www.southernliving.com)

Whatever you do to your container garden let it reflect your personality. Add collectibles to your containers, use an old chest of drawers and plant in the drawers, use inexpensive figurines to set off your plants in the container. The sky is the limit!

Chapter 3

CONTAINER GARDEN ESSENTIALS

Container gardens are highly versatile and manageable. You can grow ornamental and edibles in containers of just about any shape or size. You do need to follow several essential tips and tricks to keep your container garden growing and looking beautiful. It is easy to care for a container garden, just remember they require extra watering and feeding, lots of sunlight, and pruning.

Watering, Pests and Fertilizer

Water your container gardens frequently. Potting soil dries out much quicker than regular garden soil and in really hot weather you may have to water more than once a day. If you let your vegetables go dry just one time, you may stunt the growth of your vegetables and spoil the harvest.

Stick your finger in the soil. This is the easiest way to determine if your container garden needs water. If the top few inches of soil are dry, you need to water. Tip the container on its side. If the soil is dry the container will be lighter.

Vegetable container garden and watering system (www.urganorganicgardener.com)

Water thoroughly. Wetting dry potting soil is a bit different than watering a regular garden. The root ball of the plants may shrink a bit and pull away from the side of the pot as the soil dries. You may find that the water slushes down the side of the container and doesn't wet the soil. To prevent this problem fill the top of the pot with water more than once so the root ball can absorb the water and begin to expand. Do avoid overwatering, however. (You can tell if you have overwatered if the water starts to flood over the sides of the container and run quickly though the drainage holes in the bottom. Stop watering at that point.)

Good water drainage is vital for container gardens. If you are using a container that does not have a hole in the bottom, put coarse materials in the bottom of the container. This will keep the plants' roots out of excess water.

Note that putting gravel in the bottom of a pot with holes does nothing to ensure good drainage. Water naturally flows toward inner material not away from it. Large air spaces between pieces of gravel will not help with drainage. Gravel or clay shards just prevent soil from exiting though the holes.

Fertilize frequently. Nutrients are leached from the soil when you frequently water container gardens. Fertilize your plants at least every two weeks. You can use a liquid or water-soluble fertilizer to get your plants the best nutrients right down to the roots. Find organic fertilizers if you can.

Watch out for pests. Container grown plants have fewer pest problems since they are generally isolated from other plants. Sterilized potting soil does not have disease spores and insects are not lying in wait just to jump on your plants. However, if you do find pests, get rid of them quickly so your whole container is not wiped out.

Chapter 4

The Right Soil is Crucial

When developing a container garden all you need to do is fill pots with soil, stick in the plants and add more soil. Give it some water and viola! you have a container garden. It's almost that easy. Tricks that will help your container garden stay gorgeous, grow healthy vegetables and awesome flowers, plus save you money are:

- Avoid filling your container with soil straight from the garden. Even if your garden is so very wonderful and has the very best soil that money can buy, garden soil is too heavy for containers. It is also too full of weed seeds, bugs and eggs, bacteria and other gunk, plus it will not drain properly. Use potting soil or potting mix or container mix. Potting soil is aerated, sterile, and lightweight in addition it is made from organic materials and mineral particles. Potting soil is really soilless; it doesn't really contain any dirt.

- You can get potting soil in bulk if you need. Tryout different brands to discover which ones you like the best. Don't' worry about choosing the wrong potting soil. Plants will love it no matter what brand you purchase.

- Be aware that you will need a great deal of potting soil, but you don't need to fill the pot to the top. Most vegetable roots only go 10 to 12 inches into the soil. If you add more than that you are wasting potting soil. A good trick is to put plastic soda and milk bottles in the bottom of your container. Throw in the soil. The container will be light and easy to move and you are recycling. You have "killed two birds with one stone", plus you are saving money and being "green."

- Don't use the same soil year after year. Planting in the same soil from last year will not be good for your plants. Soil nutrition gets depleted and the soil probably has undiscovered diseases, fungal spores and insects. Just throw the old potting soil in your regular ground garden. Clean out your pots, wash out with water, and refill with this year's soil.

Container Gardening

Self-watering containers (kriscarr.com)

If you are truly an environmentalist, make your own potting soil. Combine a bit of dirt, some aged compost and a handful of sand. By making your own potting soil you have complete control over your plants. This will be a great, inexpensive medium for your garden seedlings, container gardens or house plants. Making your own potting soil gives you the opportunity to choose your own nutrients and you can avoid using commercial chemicals. A good potting soil is easy to handle, drains well, and contains a great deal of organic matter.

Chapter 5

Homemade Potting Soil Recipe

Use the right soil and this is what you get! (www.botanical-journeys-plant-guides.com)

For homemade potting soil, add a little bit of garden soil to add density plus is already available. However, do not use garden soil containing pesticides, chemical fertilizer residues or environmental pollutants. Solarize your common garden soil by covering a pile of garden soil with clear, plastic sheeting for four to six weeks. Covering your garden soil with plastic will kill weed seeds, pests and pathogens. You can also sterilize your garden soil in your oven or microwave, but this methods takes a long time and is, well, dirty.

You next need compost. Compost contains beneficial microbes and has a great water-holding capacity and nutrient content. If you make compost yourself, you have a free supply. Make sure it is fully decomposed and screened into a small and consistent size.

Add sand to your mix. Coarse builder's sand improve drainage, add weight to the mix and provides physical support for roots and growing plants.

You will need sphagnum peat moss. Peat moss is a stable ingredient that take s a long time to break down. It is very inexpensive and bulks up mixes without adding weight. It holds water well.

Composed pine bark lightens up soil mixes. It increases pore sizes and allows air and water to travel freely. It is very slow to break down, but beware, pine bark can rob nitrogen from the soil.

Perlite or volcanic rock is heated to become a lightweight and sterile addition to potting soil. It holds three to four times its weight in water and increases pore spaces. Drainage is improved with perlite. You can use perlite in place of sand if you prefer.

Making your own soil for container gardening onehundreddollarsamonth.com

Add vermiculite to your mix. Vermiculite is a mined mineral that is conditioned by heating. It expands into light particles is used to increase the porosity of soil mixtures. Vermiculite adds calcium and magnesium to the soil. Be careful when handling vermiculite, it does contain asbestos.

Limestone is necessary to adjust the pH of soil mixes that have sphagnum peat or composited pine bark.

You will also need additional nutrient sources if your soil mixture does not contain compost. Natural fertilizers that come from mined minerals, animal byproduct or manures are perfect. A combination of natural fertilizer provides a stable and eco-friendly source of nutrients. Your organic fertilizer blend should contain combinations of alfalfa meal, blood meal, bone meal, cottonseed mean and crab meal. Look for fertilizers with fish meal, greensand, kelp meal and dehydrated manures plus rock phosphate.

If you are mixing large quantities of potting soil, you can use a cement mixer or compost tumbler. Mix very thoroughly so you product is consistent.

General Potting Soil Mix
6 Gallons of sphagnum peat moss
¼ cup limestone
4 1/4 gallons vermiculite or perlite
4 1/4 gallons of compost.
Mix together 2 cups of rock phosphate, 2 cups of greensand, and ½ cup of bone mean. Mix in 4 ¼ gallons of compost. Mix 2 cups of rock phosphate, 2 cups of greensand, and ½ cup of bone meal. Add ¼ cup kelp meal, mix, and add 1 ½ cups to your general potting mix.

Use your newly developed potting soil quickly. Avoid storing it to prevent the nutrients from floating away.

Chapter 6

Planting a Container Garden

A colander container, and some funky decorations (homehardware.ca)

Plant Strawberries in a container and keep it indoors or out. (dougoster.com)

A container garden is a living flower or vegetable arrangement. Keep your container garden looking and growing great by making sure the roots are healthy and the foliage gets enough sunlight. One type of plant in a container is the simplest to maintain, but plants that thrive in like soil with the same watering and light conditions can make successful combinations.

The plants that are most suitable for container gardening are the ones that can grow in small spaces. Dwarf or those plants that bear fruit over a longer period of time are also good. Read the information on the vegetables you want to plant. Most tomatoes, peppers, cucumbers, squash and eggplants require full sun and containers can be placed in sunny areas. You can grow leafy vegetable like lettuce, cabbage, collards, mustard greens, spinach and parsley in more shady areas. Root vegetables like turnips, beets, radishes, carrots and onions will grow in shady conditions, and most herbs will perform well in full sun or partial shade locations.

Choose a theme when planting a container garden. This will give your container garden an organized look and feel. Consider complementary colors and the back ground where you will leave your container. Just choose your favorite colors and mix and match. Any combination will look awesome. Follow the color wheel or just use your imagination. Mother Nature isn't picky about the colors she puts together, so why should you be?

You do need to think about the lighting, don't put shade loving plants together with sun worshipers. This would be a disaster. Pick plants that have similar requirements. For example, plants that thrive in dry climates have thick and waxy leaves to hold moisture. Their roots like to dry out between waterings. Add them together in one container. Grow different succulents together, and they will provide an awesome artistic garden for you.

Chapter 7

VEGETABLES IN A CONTAINER

You can grow vegetable in contains from large pots to five gallon buckets or half barrels. Plant a single tomato plant or several small vegetables like broccoli or cabbage. Pick out dwarf or bush forms of tomatoes, pumpkins, and winter squash. They are most suited to container gardening. Avoid the pumpkins or tomatoes or winter squash that will grow to huge sizes, they might break your containers.

Salad garden in a container (greenerlifes.com)

Plant a salad container garden. Use different lettuces, cherry tomatoes, parsley or chives. Add a cucumber plant for interest. Plant a pizza garden with basil, tomatoes and peppers. You can also plant container that have edible flowers like pansies, nasturtiums and marigolds.

Plants that only grow for one season are annual plants and these container gardens only last for one season. Annual plants are awesome in containers. Look for those plants that love the warm weather and bloom all summer. Geraniums, marigolds, begonias, scarlet sage and nicotiana are wonderful choices. There are many more annual plants that are awesome in container gardens. Experiment. The beauty of a container garden; if one plant doesn't work, pull it out and plant another type.

Perennial container gardens are those planted with hardy perennials and shrubs that will grow from year to year and season to season. Hostas and daylilies are good perennial container plants. You can also try European wild ginger, ferns, sedges, lavender and sedums. Ornamental grass works well in containers as do dwarf conifers.

Chapter 8

SEEDS IN A CONTAINER GARDEN

You can plant any type of seed in a container garden. You just need to read the package to determine the water, sunlight and soil needs. However if you are using a container garden to grow seedlings for transplanting in your outside ground garden, there are different techniques.

Containers should be at least three inches deep with small drainage hole. You can use plastic containers or plastic plant pots or even half-gallon milk cartons cut lengthwise. Purchase a good quality seed starting mix that is available from a good nursery or garden center. Add water to the seed starting mix and combine. Your soil needs to be thoroughly moistened before you fill the containers. Fill the container to an inch below the top and tap it to settle the mix. Make a seed furrow about ¼ inch deep and drop in an individual seed. Make sure the seeds are an inch a part. Sprinkle starting mix to fill the furrows and pat firmly but gently. Use a spray bottle to water the seeds.

Love lettuce? Plant in a container! (www.ellenogden.com)

As your seedlings sprout, watch them and move them to a warm and sunny spot. Keep the containers moist and watered. When your seeds have given you seedlings that are about 3 inches tall and have leaves, move them to a deeper container so they have room to grow. If you have planted seeds in a container you are going to use, your job is done. Just move them into position.

Chapter 9

CARING FOR YOUR CONTAINER GARDEN

Beginning container gardeners, expert gardeners, or master gardeners; it doesn't matter. There are specific tips you need to follow to keep your container garden looking awesome all season long.

Double container (urbanext.illinois.edu)

Make sure the draining is adequate. Keeping your plants adequately watered, but not drowning is a matter of life and death of a plant. If there aren't enough holes for water to drain out of your pot, the soil becomes too wet and the roots rot. Drill or punch holes in your pot if you need. Adding gravel, shards or stones to the bottom of your container garden does not increase drainage. Unless you are the perfect container gardener caretaker, you need drainage holes.

- Check out the light. Place your container (without plants) where you want it to grow and watch how much sun hits it. Then plant the plants that either love lots of sun or move your pot to a shadier space.

- Potting soil has no accessible nutrients for plants. You need to add those nutrients. You need to add fertilizer directly to your soil. Use a slow release fertilizer to your potting mix. Mix up a big batch in a bucket or fill or pot with soil and mix in the fertilizer. Organic potting soil and organic fertilizers used together are the best. Fertilize every week or two with a liquid fertilizer. Fish emulsion seaweed blend is perfect. It might smell terrible, but plants love it.

- Before you run off to the nursery to buy plants make a list. Greenhouses are wonderful places, but they are also overwhelming. If you find yourself just standing in the doorway wondering what plants you want, you will be there for hours and the joy of planting will have to wait. You should know where you are placing your pots. Head for the sun plants, or the shade plants. If really get into a bind, ask a nursery worker.

- Save the plant tag. Tags let you know how big your plant will grow, how much light and water it needs or when to fertilize. The tag also tells you if your plant is annual or perennial. Tags also give you information about a plants traits or how it is shaped and how it will grow.

- Don't cry if your plants die. Sometimes they do. Known when to give up on a plant in a container. When a plant starts looking sick you can cut it back dramatically and hope for the best. May plants just need a haircut and will grow back wonderfully. However if you have a plant with signs of disease, take it out and put in a new plant. This is why nurseries are open all summer ... so you can replant.

- Harden or acclimate your plants. This is a tedious process, but it will help your plants thrive. Move them gradually into the sun, water them sparingly, and expose them to the elements over a period of time.

Chapter 10

DEALING WITH CONTAINER GARDEN PROBLEMS

Container gardening is very popular and there are so many ways you can plant a container garden within your available space. When you first plant or buy your container garden it is awesome, beautiful and perfect. However, plant space is so tight in a container garden; there is less margin for error. Take care of problems as they crop up instead of just hoping planting issues will go away. (Don't just add water and fertilizer to an overcrowded container. Prune, pull, and replant those plants that are looking strangled.)

Common Problems

Tall and spindly plants with little or no production of flowers or vegetables is a problem caused by insufficient light. You may need to augment the sunlight with artificial lighting. If possible, move the container into a sunny spot.

Container garden growing, well, ugly. (www.organizedclutter.net)

Stunted vegetable plants are distressing and if this problem appears in your container garden you may have a low level of phosphate in the soil. Change to a fertilizer with a high phosphate level to correct this problem. Phosphate will help your plants bloom in a limited space.

Plants in a container garden may appear listless and wilted. The problems may be as simple as insufficient watering. Additional watering may help the plants bloom and produce. You may also have inadequate drainage in the soil causing the roots of your plants to get too much water. Check to ensure that the drainage holes in the container are not clogged or blocked with sediment.

Plants in a container garden can appear yellow. If they do, this is excess moisture in your container garden. Re-evaluate the amount of water at scheduled waterings, and check the drainage holes in the container. Make a note of your fertilizing schedule. Inadequate fertilization also causes yellow leaves.

Chapter 11

MISTAKES TO AVOID

As easy and wonderful as container gardening can be, you can do things that will cause you to regret your decision to garden in a container.

Don't add soil and plants to your large container if you are planning to move it to a different spot. One you have filled a container with dirt and plants, it will be overwhelmingly heavy. Place your large pot in the same place where it will live and then plant it. Your back will thank you.

Avoid over watering and drowning your plants. Use containers that have drainage holes. You can never have too many drainage holes. Measure the moisture requirements for your plants and follow directions to the tea. Before you water, check if the soil is moist. If you over water the leaves of your plants may turn yellow and fall off or your plants could get very limp. You can move your container garden into a sheltered spot to dry out if you need.

Coleus, eaten and starving (www.corgnaizedclutter.net)

Avoid under watering. Container gardens need water at least once a day in the heat of the summer. If you have hanging plants or small containers they may need to be watered twice a day. These types of container gardens hold less soil and thus less moisture. Really soak your plants, but again don't drown them.

One annoying mistake that is awkward is plant to pot ratio. Consider the proportions of your plants to the container. A large container filled with short plants will look silly. Try to plant at least one plant that is as tall as the container. Use plants that spill over the sides. Experiment but don't keep all the plants the same size.

When purchasing plants for your container garden, look for healthy plants. Go to a reputable local nursery to start your quest for healthy plants. Box stores may have awesome plants, but they might be diseased and unhealthy. Ask the gardener if they will help you pick out appropriate plants for you container garden.

When your container garden starts to look leggy, and it will, cut plants back. If they are looking too tired and overdone, put them in an out-of-the-way spot until they rebound. Give them a good haircut and they will be healthy and happy.

Don't starve your plants. Potting mixes have very few nutrients that plants need. Add those nutrients to the soil. Read labels. Use fertilizers for flowers plants on ornamentals. Vegetables and herbs require their own special types of fertilizers.

Avoid having unrealistic expectations. When planning a container garden, think about what you are doing in the summer. If you travel quite a bit get self-watering containers or an automatic drip system. It is always a good idea to garden how you live. If you are formal you may want to plant container gardens in specific ways and colors. If you are casual, just plant how you like. Most container gardeners love big and overflowing containers with lot of colors and blossoms. Grow vegetables and herbs galore in a container garden. The best advice from gardeners is to have fun with however you garden.

Repotting

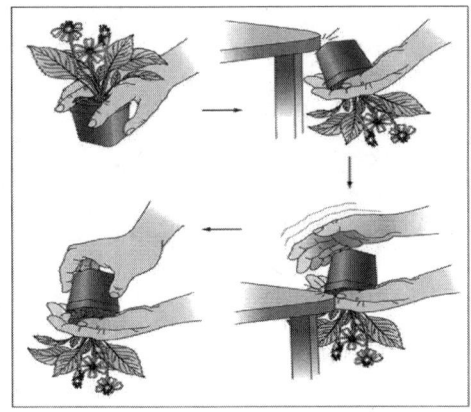

Indoor kitchen garden (www.allmodern,com)

Correct technique for removing a pant from its pot (www.dummies.com)

Most healthy container garden plants outgrow their posts. All you need to do to reinvigorate a root bound plant is to repot it in a bigger pot.

Recognize when it is time to repot. If soil drains out quickly or is degraded, roots protrude from drainage holes, and water sits on the soil surface too long after watering are a few of the signs that say, "re-pot me." Think a plant looks top heavy or as if it is going to break the pot? Get a bigger pot.

The best time to repot most plants is when they are growing in the spring or summer. But if you are a gardener who schedules repotting and repots in the fall, that is great, too.

- Get the plant out of its pot. Water the root ball thoroughly in advance. Invert the pot and support the top of the root ball with your hand. Literally pull the root ball and plant out of the smaller pot. You may have to knock the edge of the pot against a sturdy surface. Be careful not to break your pot.

- The plant ready for reporting should slid out with the root ball and soil in one piece. If soil falls free of the roots, you may not need to repot. Look for white or light colored roots. If you have black or foul smelling roots, these are signs of fungal diseases. Unless you are terribly attached to the plant, you might want to put it on the compost heap.

- Trim the roots and loosen up the root ball before replanting. A sharp knife or pruning shears are perfect for this job. Make about three or four vertical cuts a third of the way up the root ball. If you have roots growing in a circular pattern, cut through them. This will prevent the plant from strangling itself. Roots that are thick along the sides of the root ball need to be shaved or peeled away. Gently untangle the root ball with your fingers.

- To prevent soil from leaking out the bottom of the new pot, cover the drainage hole with a coffee filter or pot shard. Don't use gravel or charcoal in the bottom of pots. They really don't help with drainage and do take up valuable space. Make sure the pot is slightly bigger than the root ball.

- Fill with fresh potting soil and trim the top of the plant. Put a few inches of moist soil in the pot and tap it down. Plant the plant the center of the pot, and look to see if the root ball is sitting about an inch below the rim of the pot. If the plant is in the pot too deep, raise it and add more soil. If the root ball is too high, dig out some soil, or just start over.

- Fill the space around the root ball with soil. Stuff or press soil in around the plants. If you are a filler, just fill the pot to the brim and let the soil settle in during watering. Always leave some room at the top of the pot so it can hold water.

Chapter 12

INDOOR CONTAINER GARDENS

Grow awesome flowers in an indoor container garden (www2.fiskars.com)

Nothing brightens up your home than a container garden. Use spring bulbs and for a totally wonderful spring pick-me up. Let the glorious colors and textures of your favorite flowers become key elements of your home's décor.

Bring spring indoors by pairing up Dutch hyacinths, trumpet daffodils, pink tulips and grape hyacinths in a metal or ceramic container. Find something awesome and eclectic at a flea market or antique store and just plant your heart away. Pack blubs close together to intensify their ambience. Top off your living arrangement with green moss.

Succulents are very popular and you can go wild with them in a complementary pot. Cacti have thorns, but find those that are soft and inviting. Choose tall cacti to anchor your pot and small ones to emphasize. Succulents do grow very fast, but are very awesome. Use Kalanchoe thyrsiflora, spaghetti strap agave or hope peperoni. You can find succulent potting mix at garden stores. Never use the soil from your ground garden for a succulent container garden. Garden soil contains harmful bacteria.

Figure 2 Fun indoor tomato container garden (yourorganicchild.co)

A woodsy mossy basket can hold a lush growth of plants straight out of the woodland. Doily lace cap hydrangea blooms added with bold baby ferns and vines spilling over the edge of the container are perfect for any sunny spot in your home.

Terrariums and glass plant houses are making a comeback. They are endearing, easy to take care of and just wonderful to look at. Try a rex begonia, white Anne fittonia and mosses you found on a walk, and add them to a stunning glass house or bowl. You won't regret what you have created! Just remember to mist them once a week.

Wine-colored fall container Echeveria nodulosa, Phormium "Sundowner", and Heucherella or Sweet Tea. (www.sunset.com)

Give your indoor container garden good air circulation. Pay attention to their needs and they will be happy. Take care of pest problems immediately and get to know your plants. Plants need food, water and sunlight to survive, but different plants require different treatments. Choose houseplants that thrive on the amount of light you provide. Healthy plants will ward of pests and diseases better than sick or weak plants.

Use regular fertilizer to maintain healthy growth. An all-around fertilizer can be added to your watering can. Use a fertilizer that is a balanced formula of 6-12-6 fertilizer plus humic and amino acids.

Container Gardening

Add vitamins. Fertilize house container gardens from January through September and then let them rest.

Have a watering schedule. If you alternate periods of drought and flood you will stress out your plant's root system. Most plants like moist roots, but are not fond of wet soils. You might have plants that prefer to dry out between waterings, but always check the care label. Indoor plant books will also help you determine the right watering schedule. Invest in self-watering planters to make it easier to keep your plants happily hydrated.

Us a good natural and multipurpose pest control spray. Neem oil spray is a natural potassium pest control spray and works on a wide variety of pests. It will kill scale on your houseplants and controls powdery mildew.

Indoor herb and vegetable garden (www.southernsavers.com)

Chapter 13

10 Container Garden Ideas

So many different ways to display your container gardens. You can group them, use them alone, or place them in our ground garden. Add container gardens to your porch or use them as a welcome mat. Anyway you choose will be awesome. Browse through these ten ideas to get an idea of what you can do with a container garden.

Container Gardening

Wander your local garden store, pick out the plants you love and then go for the container. Let the container extend the theme. A container garden is an instant garden.

Match icy blue plans together with warm combos of bright pinks and purples. Organize your container garden in threes for the best design. That means three containers with three plants each or one plant in three containers. Keep the sizes relevant.

Start out with a thriller, add a filler, and finish with a spiller. Gorgeous containers include calla lilies, foliage or flowering plants like lantana and geraniums, and a training plants like Livingstone daisy. Let it cascade over the edge for a gorgeous arrangement.

Sunshine Garden (www.midwestliving.com)

Figure 3Gorgeous! Lush Container Garden (www.midwestliving.com*)*

Nothing speaks drama like this awesome Sunshine in a container garden. Plants that love the sun give your yard pizazz. Use vinca vine, water hyssop, annual phlox, daisies, impatiens (New Guinea), bellflower, White monkey flower, Lobela, Gerbera Daisy, Mandevilla vine, Delphinium, Dusty Miller and Salvia (Blue Queen.) All these plants can be found in your local greenhouse they are well known and grow well in many climate zones.

Vegetables grown in bright pots to add pizazz and interest (www.bhg.com)

Check out gardening books, catalogues and green houses. Container gardening using vegetables is becoming more and more popular. You can grow your own food in fantastic containers. Try this awesome container garden of tomatoes. An increasing number of compact and dwarf varieties are being developed for small spaces.

Cherry tomatoes and basil in a hanging basket (www.bhg.com)

Pair tomato and basil together. This is a very pretty display and will be very tasty when used in your favorite Italian recipe. If you are container gardening using hanging plants, you might want to design a drip system. This is the same type os system that cities use to keep their hanging gardens gorgeous all year. Check with a garden supply store.

Get creative! Use recycled wooden boxes or anything else you have hanging around for this container garden (www.bhg.com)

Save money by using recycled containers. Old wine crates or milk boxes create an eclectic and colorful container garden. Lettuce sits side by side with Thumbelina carrots, overbearing strawberries and marigolds (yes, marigolds are eatable).

Anything that can hold soil can be a container garden. This awesome container garden is a living centerpiece that can go outside or indoors.

Modern look, using aluminum garbage cans. It might be bet to purchase new cans that haven't been used (Courtesy of Brian Patrick Flynn)

How to Grow Practically Everything

@2010 Dorling Kindersley Limited

Just use whatever you have around to plant a container garden. New aluminum garbage cans filled with spider plants and taller salvia and vining pansies make an impression against the brick of this home. Notice the containers are on wheels for ease of moving. If you are using containers this large, note that using plastic bottles as inside drainage instead of rocks will keep things light and moveable.

Really neat carry-along succulents can be moved anywhere you want. An old metal tool toe makes a perfect home for these succulents. Drill drainage holes in the boot, don't overwater and enjoy. Plant with different types of succulents.

Drawers and shelving as a container garden (themicrogardener.com)

4www.diynetwork.com

Recycle your old furniture by turning it into a container garden. You can do just about anything you like if you have imagination. Wooden drawers set on a ladder framework forms a great space for a container garden.

Chapter 14

TIPS FOR SUCCESSFUL CONTAINER GARDENING

- Purchase sterilized soil for use in your containers. This will ensure the potting soil is free from weed seeds and diseases.

- Look out for weeds such as the onion weed and yellow nutsedge. One these weeds are established they are almost impossible to get rid of.

- Grouping garden pots is better and more effective visually and practically than scattering containers around your yard.

- Water late in the afternoon when evaporation is less.

- Add fertilizer and plant foods tick on a scheduled basis.

- Repot plants when they outgrow the container.

- Choose the right size container for your pot plants. If you are using large pots, first choose where you want them to reside, and then fill with soil and plants. Carting spoil-filled containers is not easy.

- Use organic mulch to discourage weed growth and encourage surface roots.

Any container will work! (www.landscape-and-garden.com)

Plants are light sensitive. Before moving your plants from a shady to a sunny location, prepare them by moving them gradually. This will "toughen" up your plants and prevent sun burn.

WAIT! – DO YOU LIKE FREE BOOKS?

My **FREE Gift** to You!! As a way to say **Thank You** for downloading my book, I'd like to offer you more **FREE BOOKS!** Each time we release a NEW book, we offer it first to a small number of people as a test–drive. Because of your commitment here in downloading my book, I'd love for you to be a part of this group. You can join easily here → http://gardening-mastery.com/

CHECK OUT THESE #1 BEST SELLING BOOKS FROM JOY LOUIS!

http://www.amazon.com/Joy-Louis/e/B00UMOZJE6

Conclusion

Thank you again for downloading this book!

If you enjoyed this book, then I'd like to ask you for a favor, would you be kind enough to leave a review for this book on Amazon? It'd be greatly appreciated!

Help us better serve you by sending questions or comments to greatreadspublishing@gmail.com–Thank you

Made in the USA
Middletown, DE
07 March 2016